IN MEMORY OF DAVID ARCHER

IN MEMORY OF
DAVID ARCHER

by

George Barker

FABER AND FABER
3 Queen Square
London

First published in 1973
by Faber and Faber Limited
3 Queen Square London WC1
Printed in Great Britain by
Western Printing Services Ltd Bristol
All rights reserved

ISBN 0 571 10398 7

TO SEBASTIAN

To lift a hand
to those who have gone before us
those friends and
oddfellows to whom
only death can restore us
(I have heard
as in day dreams
them calling sometimes for us
out of a silence that seems
like a dead chorus)
to lift a hand in farewell
for them at the black bell
neither you David nor I
found this a hard thing to do –
for they, most of them, died
in a sort of twisted pride
or as they lifted up
the whiskey in the cup
or turning a handsome head
in honour among the dead
so that, with the wave
of a hand toward the grave
you and I, as they went
down out of the present,
could seem to call:
'Stand up and speak well
in the empty hall
of heaven or empty hell
for us all'.
But, David, I am at
such a loss, such a loss
that I cannot, I can not

lift a hand or a word
as you descend
the under ground
and one way stair
to that dead end
where
the friend is found.
Are you there
now? Dear friend
it does not matter where
you are for better or
worse where you are
there can be there
no more of the withering
belief (O withering arm
and withering leaf!)
or the withering Upas tree
of life,
no more ever again
of that pain.
The decent dirt
David unlike the lovers
will not desert you nor
the grave stone hurt
you but with love convert
you into stone, into
the dust and earth
of which both life and death
know the worth.
The dark streets at night
echoing our tread
seem for a moment bright
with what we said
and what we might
even have done, but the light

or dream of those times
is gone
and it was not done.
The familiar vision faded
and is forgotten in
our failure, so degraded
that ideal by
our delusion, so humiliated
we by what we knew
was both foregone and fated,
that in the end
what you saw, my friend,
was that life itself
was the vision
that you hated.
All the gifts of red
roses and blank
cheques and bed
fellows grew rank
and went bad
and you and they
sank down in the grey
ends of a day
that stank as it died
in the guttering
palace. I think
that all you leave
behind you in the evening
is a darkened room
empty save for old
newspapers and cigarette ends
and in the gloom
the enormous gold
urn of your heart
in which lie the ashes of your friends.

I have no hope that I shall ever see the
rainbowing archipelagos. Nor do I wish that
some day, somehow, I may. Let them flash their
sunsetting effigies in the evening seas as
I walk in this day.

Long, long the memory in its exile wanders
over those fields of forget me nots and morning
everlasting glories where, wheeling and silent,
the eagles and vultures and entrail devouring angels
hover in the air.

These poems are offered up
   to your memory, David, like
those votive souvenirs
   at old wishing wells, where we
come of an autumn evening
   with blowing clouds and rain
and a cold wind from nowhere
   that lashes the winter tree
   beside the wishing well.
And from its brittle branches
   our credulous offerings
squeak and flounce and swivel
   and flap in the nowhere wind:
the doll with no eyes, a glove,
   a bottle of Gordon's gin,
a flower, a bit of old rag and
   this verse in other words.

The life I shed upon the ground
   looks up at me, looks up at me
   and in its scarlet lake I see
my face of yesterday lying drowned
   and smiling as in sleep it seems
   cradled among rocks and dreams
of what will never be.

Early in the dawns of May
   under the Medusa tree
   I shall stand and you will see
my transfigured head of day
   hanging in a bleeding dream
   as the serpents hiss and scream
and eat eternity away.

I think that like many susceptible men
I have collected several monsters that might
– had I not fed them flesh again & again –
very much better have been buried when
    they first came to light.

Six doves and a small bunch of early spring
crocuses, a primrose and a rare
Siberian primula I received this morning
persuade me that the little pretty thing
    calls for no less a care.

VI

I have seen men who behaved as though they were invisible
surprised to find that we know, nevertheless,
that they are here. They had rendered themselves
invisible in order to produce certain effects
and we detected their presence by these effects.
Similarly the presence of the god can often
be suspected because no other reasonable
explanation than this presence could account for
the ridiculous behaviour of phenomena.
If I insist that no men are invisible, what
in truth I am saying is, simply: 'I
object to the fact that invisible men
cannot be seen. I cannot see such men.
Therefore they are not there. There are no
invisible men.' And at this point I find
I have been dreaming. Then suddenly and
fearfully it comes over me that in the order
of dreams many men and many other things
are only too invisible. I dreamed
I held a rose in my hand. I woke, and the rose
was there. I held the rose in my hand.
I dreamed that no rose was there. I awoke
and found no rose in my hand.

The flying fishes drip with fire as
    I gaze at them. The rose turns
into a labyrinth of dust and
    ashes as the sunset burns.

In those October evenings when
    the soul dreads what it believes,
I hear one drop of blood again
    and again drip upon the leaves.

VIII

I cannot see. The place I do not know.
Who is that person standing by the wall?
Why do you ask the date on which I died?
Where is the house to which I am asked to go?
What was the question you put to me when
I happened to be listening to that child
Crying for god knows what outside the door?
Who is it calling me again and again
From my own chamber like a person lost?

I hear the dead man calling from the desert
But never the love, never the love, never.
I saw you. I saw you there. You were the other
Side of that window always hidden in shadow.
I cannot see. The place is not the place where
I was supposed to be. Who are those people
Whispering, with heads together, in the corner?
Why do they speak when they should be silent?

I think that I see, walking in the moonlight
The Magus Zoroaster and my dead father
Talking together. What is this heartbroken
House? Is this my home? Why do you look at me
As though I had no parents? Who is at the window?
You? It is you? I saw you pass, your hand
Covering your face in shadow, and, in the moonlight,
Falling, seven wounds, like stars.

IX

I hear the children crying in the infanticidal night
I hear the wild wind blowing till it blows the cold moon
    white
I see morning gathering up the leaves to bury them from
    sight
And the doves and Mercy silent in the forest.

Where were you Lamp that always burns within the darkest
    wood?
The Parson said: What happens always happens for the good.
There, looking on with winter eyes, the will of God just
    stood
And the doves and Mercy silent in the forest.

Where were you Christian Andersen? Or Mary, where were
    you
When these two babes together lay down and the cold wind
    blew?
The Will of God, that cold cold wind, blew through them
    through & through,
And the doves and Mercy silent in the forest.

These little ones, these pretty ones, they're luckier than
    most.
And now not even fate can find these two forever lost
Beside a bush beneath a tree covered with snow and frost,
And the doves and Mercy silent in the forest.

Having at last seen through the appearance of things
I can reveal that somewhere on the far side of reality
hangs a notice board which reads: 'The Everyman Moral
   Steeple Chase.
Starting Point Here'.

And because I have quite outgrown childish things
I am no longer afraid of the dark.
Now I am afraid of something even more childish:
the gods of darkness.

Thus when I reflect on the intervention of chance in our
   affairs
I am left with the simpleminded conviction
that it can only be an alternative term
for the irony of these gods.

I saw the mad child sitting by
   the river as it ran.
I heard her singing quietly
'This river sprang out of the eye
   and the grief of man.

'Those songs are silent now, but I
   sing up for the mute swan,
the dumb fish, the dead child and
   the dirty soul of man.'

And over those years, for me and for my brother and sisters,
the spectre, worse than the spectre of war over Europe,
of my parents' poverty. My mother every Wednesday
pawning her wedding ring and the blankets from her bed, my
father returning at evening to the three small tenement
rooms and his family of seven, a twist of drawn
exhaustion in his face that we knew concealed
the fact that once again no job had turned up.

So that, as a child, I watched, day by day,
but without knowing it, the soul of a proud man
being slowly and mercilessly torn out of his body
and thrown to the dogs in the gutter. His children knew
that the last glint of this pride somehow or other
slept in the Army pistol he kept under his pillow.

By what natural act of faith do we awaken
in the morning? By what act of faith do we surrender
ourselves to the suspension of this faith at night?
By this same natural act of faith we live our lives
in a series of commonplace spiritual affirmations
instead of disappearing in a thin puff of smoke
each time we light a match. The purpose of my life
is to pursue this natural act of faith until it brings
me to the Gates of Paradise. These Gates we have also
    constructed
out of our affirmations. This is all really no odder
than playing clock golf on the moon.

Images! Venerable as Druidical trees,
pockmarked, meaningless, daubed with woad
and spit and sperm like mistletoe, they sit,
the old gods of the imagination
presiding over the woods of the intellect
with a power drawn from sources far too deep
for the axe to reach. Like wounds they provide
an egress through which the lifeblood can escape
and the atavistic memories return. All images
transcend their own specifications simply
because they involve all other images, just as
the nexus of individual existence involves
all of us in a sort of infinitely
complex and singular law of effects. Thus it is that
the Yarmouth windmill seen by a dirty pond
from which the skeleton of an old bicycle points
up at the sky, this may call up from the memory
a day when we dreamed of death by exhaustion in
the illusions of Hither Arabia. What law operates here?
It is the law of Medusa's antitheses, so
that every image carries all other images
on its small back in an ascending order
until, at the top, there sits the opposite
and contradiction. St George gives birth to The Dragon.

Mademoiselle Desirée lounges in front of me on the champs
    fête grass
stark naked save for her net stockings, fashionable Parisian
    legs crossed,
twiddling her left nipple as she squirms on her arse:
I stare into her green Pigalle eyes and I am lost.

What I cannot see as I devour this delicious Morgan
le Fay is the set of tigershark teeth located
invisibly within the lips of her sexual organ
like a carnivorous mantrap deliciously set and baited.

Myself I am a simple materialist and the stuff
in which I believe is flesh. It manufactures love
the way the winter tree manufactures spring leaves
or clouds rain, that is, as a fact of its nature.
The body of flesh itself is, for this reason,
as strange and as sacred as that bit of baked dough
the eucharist to a fanatical catholic. It is
the temple and tabernacle of Joe Smith and
contains the Eleusinian Mysteries of Love.

I have far less reason to believe in the existence
of DNA than in the existence of this love, because
I myself have never seen a single twist of DNA but
this morning I rose from a tangled bed in which Venus
lay sleeping with newborn Eros in her arms.

What shadows and what wings
cast that vision in sleep
over this dreaming child?
Yes, I believe visionary
because through clouds and a dim
hope that hang round the ringed
globes of her shadowing brows
the dove can be perceived.
She lies there in glimmering
constructions of evening light
and over her butterfly folded
eyelids and the haunted
nenuphar of her being
the dove and four guardians hover.
And in their illumination
at one instantly vanishing moment
I see what, without knowledge
of either evil or good,
and what, with no other impulse
than to dream out existence,
the heart of man could be.
All things, then, would seem
to breathe and to be in a deep
consecration from which
the child of the altering sky
never awakened, but like
a fallen asteroid lay
in the foam laced and cradling
seas of natural existence,
out of shadow and among the
mysterious great deeps gleaming
with a glitter of heavenly

origins. I could beseech
the powers and the guardians
to let the child sleep on
in such a dream for ever
and never waken. O that
birth like the kiss of death
could suspend the smiling
child in unending and
deathless sleep, with only
the dreams of the spirit praising
the highest power for ever
and never waken. O shadowing
eve of the dove and
hovering wing of the dove,
about her in the air
of this midsummer evening
hang your occluding
and far fathering brightness
so that no dawn of day or
of life or human love
may ever again awaken
the seven sleeping sisters
the seven stars of heaven
or this child of the sky.

If the heart did not know it was a heart
it would turn instantly into a small lump of meat
and cease to beat. But the heart
believes that its duty is to beat and therefore it does.
Similarly we know it is our duty to love and
we do so simply because we possess the faculty,
and therefore we do so. For this reason
newborn monkeys mistake for their mothers the
   monstrous figures
constructed out of rags and goggles by mad zoologists.

Let us dismiss at once the metaphysical comedy of birth.
You were born into a world supremely unconscious of the
    fact that
it was brought into existence simply by your advent,
as, now, it remains supremely unaware that one day
you propose to undo it by the simple act of secession.
How many of the beautiful creatures not of the imagination,
friends invented solely to populate our loneliness,
– fictitious inhabitants of an ignominious biography –
understand that they have only us to blame for
the miseries and splendours we precipitated them into?

XX

Mother O Mother, what is that star
  Like a nail in the sky?
My little babe, it is only the candle
  I see you by.

Mother O Mother, what is this wound
  I feel here at my side?
My little babe, it is only the straw
  You lie beside.

Mother O Mother, what is the thorn
  I feel here at my brow?
My little babe, it is only a rose
  On a small bough.

Mother O Mother, what is this love
  That tears me apart?
My little babe, it is only the shake and
  Sob of my heart.

Mother O Mother, do not weep.
  I see the bright star
And the nail and the wound and the crown rise up over
  All things that are.

Why, when we are born, do the attendant figures
– the furies, the affections, the faculties and the underpaid
   G.P.'s –
why do they abstain from strangling the babe in its cradle?

Can it be because human suffering is, in the event,
the obverse hideosity of praise, like those disgusting
oblations once offered by Aztecs to their obscene deities?

The memories of other mornings
   rise and flash within the mind
until its glass and cloudy houses
   crowd with what was left behind.
I see the child dance under water
   with dead flowers in its hand
and, once again a ragamuffin
   the bones that lie upon the sand.

Charley, are you there still, Charley?
   Who's banging on the backyard door?
I hear the dogs of childhood whining
   to scramble at my heel once more:
and in the parks the sleeping sisters
   lying in their crumpled frocks
rise from the grave and shake the death like
   leaves out of their tangled locks.

What, my heart, is the wind crying?
   I cannot see the morning sky.
Across the night I hear replying
   the sheeted hobnobbers on high:
they hide and, homeless in the darkness,
   howl like dogs that cannot go
back to the cloudy houses where we
   lived and died so long ago.

Who can be expected to compose his own elegant obituary
with the children of his loins banging at the door?
Even ingenious foxes, when they make love, trust one another
if only for the moment, and even Siberian tigresses
when they dream, dream sometimes of harmless pleasures.
Only the egoist cannot truly experience love, for
this is the one mathematical formula which truly
and conclusively proves that other people exist.

And why, incidentally, has no one ever mentioned
that the simplest demonstration of the god's existence
lies in the invention of the human ego? Only a god
could have extemporised a phenomenon
at once so monstrous, so magnificent, and so very evil.

XXIV

Heavenly events of those Venetian evenings, when
with such well washed sexual pride we stalked up and down
those Chirico esplanades, shirts open to the belt, an erection
like a Guinness bottle in the trouser pocket, and a supreme
confidence like Canaletto illuminating all
that we said and did. And the gilded images of the pinnacles
and Byzantine palaces and basilicas now lie covered over
in the dead eyes of my friends where they lie
under the mulct of Scotland. How can their memories fail
to haunt those amorous piazzas with our shadows?

What a bore all those politically affiliated young men
at your Parton Street Bookshop were, David, in those
forgettable thirties. They resembled waiters
bringing one a sort of cold vichysoise Utopia
on a tin tray, and they resented violently the perversity
that makes one turn away from such a degrading dish.
The word Utopia and the idea of Utopia (and although
the word is unfashionable the idea is not) have for me
always exuded the offensive connotation of
the English Public School. It is the triumph of
that atrociously vicious misconception, the team
spirit. It sounds like a synonym for menstruation.
From it all spiritual pride, all the dignity of the
Star of Morning, all the intellectual and crystal
palaces of Alighieri and John Milton, from this
disgusting little word Utopia all these and Damnation
and Salvation too have been wholly excluded. It is the
dusty shop of the haberdasher and his secret little packets
of Tampax. The vision of Herbert George Wells
united with that of Arnold of Rugby consummate
themselves in a political idea over which the Sun
would refuse ever, I believe, to preside, or the Moon
to mourn. Why on earth go to the trouble
of setting the stars in their heavenly operations
and the planets in their circles of serenity
simply in order to decorate a picnic
held by the Engineers' Union? I do not aspire
to that Utopia. I aspire to Paradise. It
is not, in the long run, really much more absurd.

What was the aspiration and
   the new impulse that moved us then?
It was the hope that we might also
   help sweep the heart clean again.

With brooms and buckets in those mountains
   we swept and swept, but root and branch
the Tree of Time and the walls of Europe
   fell on us like an avalanche.

I saw great aspirations wildly
   shaking fists as they went under,
and the last words we tried to speak
   crushed by collapsing of thunder.

And so, my poor Higgins, you really believed that you could
   get away with it all, the Virginian ham and the small
bottle of Irish whiskey and the even more risky manoeuvre
   of filching the purse of that woman whose soul is wood
the three-faced Veritas? What Hullish dreams and delusions
   could ever have whispered so cruelly to you, 'Look,
Higgins, no hands!' and then as hesitating you stood
   there, red-handed, caught alive, on went the flood-
lights of Hammersmith Hospital and we saw the black book
   the perspex mask and oxygen tube and we knew
it was the old cold bed for you. You thought you could
   pickpocket the naked truth and nick out of the blue
that monumental and obvious labour that lies
   in every man's arms, the little matter of human love.
It will not work, Higgins, the noble error that
   degrading the First Person honours everyone else.
Until such an extremity of speech overcame you at
   last that nothing was left for you to say, except, 'Well,
I demand my come-uppance and I'll get my come-uppance
   even if I die for it. I could be happy in hell.'
And there on that scruffy bed in Skid Row your farewell
   appearance made only too clear to us
that what you were really stealing this time was a march
   into the Courts of Justice where we cannot follow
until we acknowledge that we too have stolen much
   that only a death can repay. Yet one lady knew
how perfectly honourable were your greediest pretensions
   that the lies were like sweetmeats but that you were
     always hungry
for verities that, like allergies, you could not swallow.
   And this lady, whose sheets you so wished to soil for
the most childish of reasons (just because you were angry

 at finding her bed so clean) took you & chided you
and then gave you poems. Dead bull of Hull
 why could you never believe that in spite of your sweat
and whine and wholly unjovian behaviour
 that elegant dowager Veritas was your Europa?

I expect nothing to emerge from all this save a diet of
    worms.
And yet, somewhere among the furthermost landscapes
    of the mind
the sun rises in splendour and sets without regret
every day. The purpose of emotions and ideas
seems to be to affirm the authority of their own contra-
    dictions.
To subject onself to the frivolity of self examination
in order to demonstrate the purposelessness of this opera-
    tion?
All things, it seems, come down in the existential end to
the individual spirit seeking to understand
the nature of its pain. But the last suffering lies
in the illusion of this understanding. I can no more
understand this grief than the tree understands
the apple and the leaf that I stand under.

When I leave my bed in the morning
I have no conclusive evidence
that I am not still sleeping in a dream.
At what moment, in fact, was one born?
I take it on hearsay, just as I take
the existence of stars or places I have not seen.
It is sensible to do so: it is the triumph
of the commonplace.

Thus in this garden of everyday
the First Person Singular wanders around
looking for a lavatory or reading the Daily Express
or picking its teeth because it knows
that even though it may have to leave them this evening
these gardens, no matter what, will always remain.

XXX

When we get born we skim an opera hat into the ring
and it is at once caught by the Mad Hatter
who proceeds, from then on, to be us. I still
insist I have never been born. Does the homicidal
maniac offer his victims up as praise? I
have only one enemy, which is my conscience,
and only one friend, which is yours. Ah, the surgical
excision of your winged footprint from my heart!

XXXI

What secrets, then, should the word seek to divulge?
Only such secrets as are worth speaking of? What are they?
The facts can be found written on the individual face –
the accidents at crossroads, the quarrels in Italian restaurants,
the crises of chequebooks and self-love that inscribe
the lines like lies, or cut the hieroglyphics of
disgust and gratification. They are all there, the
histories of the mask, only too plain to be seen.
What is not there in the face are the secrets that
even the man himself not wholly knows.
What are these secrets and how do we fish them up?
This is the responsible operation of the one who
elects to declare himself, just as the conscience
in the confessional seeks to drag out shrieking
into the oratory evening all the ghouls of the soul
that do not intend to be seen. They do not
intend to be seen because then, heaven help them,
they might be recognised as the daughters of music.

XXXII

When she walks in the garden
   beside the apple tree
then like a dream the old old story
   comes back to me.

What, when she pulls the apple
   down from the bough,
can I do but take the fruit
   as I do now?

Would we still walk in the garden
   with flowers under foot
if we had never eaten that
   worm & fruit?

And if we walked now in Eden
   as in a dream
how could that paradise as heavenly as
   this garden seem?

From the worm and the apple tree
   of evil understood
spring up the angel and the flowers
   of this summer wood.

Paradise is paradise
   and the world a twin star
where good & evil, like lovers,
   join because they are.

Two angels walking
   together in a wood
sang: 'Even love is evil.
   Even life is good.'

XXXIII

Ceremonies of inconsolable farewell
should be held at the seventh birthday of every child.
Kiss the rod often enough and it becomes
the plumed serpent. Joy is the only praise
truly acceptable, I believe, to the gods.
Kiss the plumed serpent often enough
and it becomes the rod. Sorrow insults the sun.
Birds, tape-recorders and poets do not
really require an attentive audience.
Can a door, or the heart, be neither open
nor shut? How shame-facedly the cunt licks
its lips, like a cat with a sore conscience.
When the Ideal Home has at last been built
it will be found to contain a cupboard for skeletons
in every bloody room. Beyond good and evil you
will find a man who looks like Adam digging up
the potatoes in his little allotment. Upon
uninhabited islands fate casts a frustrated
and malevolent eye. When roses burst into blossom
does the ground believe that it has lost them?
Sometimes I am afraid of my animating spirit.
It is also afraid of me.

XXXIV

I do not aspire to write the truth about
what I think, because I would not know
when I had written it, whether what I had written
in fact was the truth, or not. Words do not deal in the truth
– nor did the Galilean Pilate – they deal in the
more human commodity of what, for the time being,
we would like to believe is the truth. It does not follow
that because the word 'truth' exists that therefore the
    verifiable
and accomplished fact of the truth exists also.
Just as it does not follow that, because we have a name for
    them,
the Hippogryph or Pendragon Wyvern can be hunted
to death with a shotgun. Perhaps in the course of a safari
through the jungles of necessary illusions
we come upon a wild Chimera, we elevate our twelve bore,
we fire and bring down an eight foot span specimen.
But how would I know I had shot such an unlikely creature?
I do not possess a reliable description
of this unfortunate beast. The only
recognisable characteristic of my Chimeras
is that they bark like housedogs. They protect me from
    burglars.
There is a sense in which all mental operations
can be best compared with the bluish glare given off
by putrescent fish. It is the flaring up or immolation
of an always decomposing system, the system of
the self destroying intellect. For where this system
makes its grave and deathbed utterance in judgement
there the soul sings up out of a sea of fire.

Come to me daughter of terrestrial waters
    come to me.
A little cold in the ground the sheets hereafter –
    come, come to me.

Come in the foam and the kissing fish that skim
    the flying wave,
and in the tides that rise until they brim
    out of the grave.

From the far shore of nowhere, over those memories
    wide as the sea,
beyond the years and out of the sunsetting mysteries,
    come to me.

The mind flitters and flies over memories like a seabird
that fishes its sustenance up from the past. But sometimes
   this
gull dives straight downward into the jaws of the shark.
This is when the imagination is seized by an allegorical
fact or an inspiration. And the springs of my childhood
   feed fountains
I have not yet even reached, let alone drunk at.
I have also visited a country in which innocence was
acquired by experience, and in this paradise the wild
animal was king, and the child merely a premature
Old Man ignorant of what he had not yet suffered.

In the evening in the basement my brother and I,
as had become our practice, took out the foils and
after a few flourishes began to fence. He retreated
slowly, smiling, up the three stone steps. I said:
Ah like a character in an opera and advanced.
He continued to smile. I drove the sword forward and saw
very slowly, as one perceives an enormous natural
   calamity,
the unguarded point of my foil enter his right eye.
And then all motions ascended into a reality
where they occurred with a kind of paralysed and
yet exaggerated formality, like slow motion automata.
I remember that my right hand lowered the foil
and I saw my brother's right eye hanging out on
the sixteen year old bone of his cheek. I heard his
blade rattle on the stone floor of the basement. I saw
the remaining eye of his face stare at me as though
I was not there. He placed his
right hand on the iron railing and raised
his left hand to the gap in his face from which
lachrymal fluid and blood exuded like grape juice.
I think that we stood thus, without speech or movement,
for several years. And as I stood staring
at the half blind person I loved most of all
with his optical nerve hooked out and his young
hand resting on the rail, I felt the gorgon's head
rising within my own so that I could not see.
Upon this motionless scene like a Revenger's play
set upon a staircase, as though she must have known
what it was that she had always been destined
to encounter at this moment, out of her kitchen
my brother's mother then came calling: What is it?

She looked at the apples of her eyes, her no longer
schoolboys of sons, she saw the swords, the stair upon
which her own blood dripped, the hand on the rail,
the dangling eyeball, the lowered head of
the sacrificial offering, the red hand of her eldest
and halved vision of her youngest son,
and she stood still.

XXXVIII

The children at the door
the children worlds away
all knock upon my one
and only heart this day

as in the hallowed evening
I hear them haunt and cry
like souls or owls or orphans
in the October sky.

Why does the bird of dawning
weep like the midnight swan?
Here in my empty room
children and stars dance on.

In the red sky of morning
around my standing soul
they dance, the stars and children
as round a burning pole.

The intellect not continually sustained by
the contemplation of its own futility
finishes up by believing that it cannot possibly
ever have existed. Just as we are haunted by
   the dread that
God can, in truth, be mocked with impunity
because, as yet, we do not recognise that
we are already suffering the consequences
of having done so. Thus the sun is the
only god who is prepared to render himself
visible every day to me and my viper.

When at the wake and watches of
the sheeted night I lie and hear
the denizen of my soul like
a Goya jackass gibe and sneer
what most appals my staring mind
and cuts my heart like swallowed glass
is the triumphant nightmare bray
and guffaw of my soul's jackass.

In what disgusting caves of night
or ruins of the empty day
this onager and scapegoat hides
when I believe it far away
I do not know. But what I know
is that I hear it howl and sing
as, daft with flagellant delight,
it weeps my chains of suffering.

This is the creature offering up
my immolation of despair,
pain and the knowledge that the pain
drives the dove higher into air;
and tears and wounds take wing and rise
like children that sing as they die,
and this ass guffaws as I bleed
its heart out upward into the sky.

What is Mercy I have heard
this pathic jackass chant and howl,
what is Mercy as I felt
the dying flesh go cold and foul,
What is Mercy and a voice

my own, cry: 'In the living cell
I hear the idiot rejoice
and Mercy like a nurse in hell.'

As I walked down the streets of Battersea
I met a young ghost a-hurrying on:
'Whither away, O whither away, pal,
There's plenty of time for hurrying on.'

But just as he passes he takes my elbow
In his cold hand as he's hurrying on:
'Come away, pal, O come away, pal,
O come away. It's time to be gone.

'To the hills where the girls with their long hair so
    golden
Stroll by bright streams, and the birds in the air
Sing you to sleep in the long summer evening,
And for ever & ever we'll lie and dream there.'

So never you walk down the streets of Battersea
Or you'll meet the pair of us hurrying on
To that green hill and that long summer evening
Where the shades of day are lingering on.

And what shall we do if we learn at last that the
nature of things is in fact and in truth without hope
without joy and without any spiritual principle at all?
Then we will sit around on the crystal rocks of E.S.P.
inventing fables that tell of a past hesperides when
we really believed such improbables were possible.

XLIII

Every night in the dark
　　two in a bed
sleep like a double one,
　　head beside head.

The fuck is the dance of death
　　and love a very near myth,
and it's a wise heart that
　　knows who it's sleeping with.

Fare well fare well the sailors
   cruising on Friday nights
the fruity streets of Soho
   under the gory lights
gunning for beds or brandies
   or a middle-aged spectacled queer,
the roly poly all night long,
   the breakfast of a beer.

Come Friday, David, come Friday
   I think maybe I'll go
and stroll again the sleazy lanes
   of nine p.m. Soho.
And, my dear, dead David
   to find, now, where you are
I'll make straight for the sailors
   leaning against the bar.

When a woman disrobes what she bares is the next
    generation
just as lovers hold hands in order to make sure they do not
    carry Sten guns.
And it is, I understand, a zoological fact that
the man is eleven times more highly sexed than the bull;
which is why he has raped Europe oftener and betterer.
Similarly, with the advent of puberty we acquire the faculty
of committing a crime that can only be condoned by a god
or circumvented by a Family Planning Association.
Tell me, if Love is what can be seen by two blind people
when they remove their clothes, is the most remarkable
fact of erection that it operates
in direct defiance of the law of Gravity?
And so, having at last dismissed the Theological Angel,
we discover that sexual pleasure provides
satisfactions so inconsequential that they can be compared
only with the mutual masturbations of a pair
of extremely thin skinned super computers.

From here between the Twin Lakes of America
   I see her where she lies
on a bed with her knees spread and the Rosa Mundi
   opening between her thighs.

XLVII

And so the Memory, like a track running back through
   Malayan jungle
lies riddled with sabre toothed tiger traps, now, after years,
covered over with the simple and natural pity of things.
It is festooned with hissing and kissing serpents born out of
   swamps
in the gardens of Babylon, and hosts of microbes hum
and crepitate like lies everywhere. And I said:
'Not for me the round trip. The land of Pelops is not for me.'

For the inhalation with which one lives and breathes, like
the stroke of the internal combustion engine, also
infinitesimally destroys one and, bit by bit,
breath by breath
brings about, in the machineries of consequence,
an accession of inexplicable relief in the breast
of a tiny marsupial in Tasmania, or the weeping
of a wild dove somewhere in Thessaly.

How can I start at the beginning, simply carry on to
the end and then stop? What about the parting of the ways?
Some of us have even gone round the bend, down the far
    straight
and round the next bend. But it so happens that the race
finished years ago. The athletes have all gone home
removed their spikes and shoved their touselled heads into
public gas ovens. The winning post has been removed to
a dead end street where it is now employed as
a NO ENTRY signpost.

For not only are heroes born of humiliation but
so is religious passion. The humiliations of
the human affair remind us continually
of the paradise that has forsaken us,
where we were never shamed.

Legends of curious singularity haunt my recollection.
In seeking to analyse their improbabilities I find
that all of them are incidents in my own obituary.
The love affairs all culminate in kisses containing cyanide;
the visionary and unvisited cities all rise into the air
like Chinese palaces and disappear; intentions,
morally admirable intentions die in deserts of pure accidie;
self knowledge, contemplating itself in Canadian lakes
finally casts itself into those depths of indulgence and
    delusion;
the bird with four feathers discovers all doves are white.

O Master not then to me speak
    or to the Angel standing
here at my side, my grave and pride,
    my love and understanding:
but let me find the word like wings
    asleep upon the Sea,
as silent as the dawn that brings
    my Kingdom come to me.

There is a state of consciousness we all experience
about ordinary objects, when they seem, every one of them,
even the empty matchbox on the mantelpiece,
to stand surrounded by an incandescent luminosity or ring
of extraordinary light, and we know then that all things,
particularly the most commonplace, exist in
the transfigured glimmering of the Holy Grail.
This illumination, then, that things emit or give off
seems to resemble the reflection of
our awareness of their inherent transcendent.
This is the theology of objects. Nor is this a matter
of probability or improbability. It is not the
essential unlikelihood of their existence that endows them
with this illumination, for no one thing can be truly
said to be less or more probable than any other.
What shines forth from the phenomenon of objects is
their simple and at the same time supernatural
joy in having achieved existence. They are congratulating
themselves on having transcended the first condition
of all natural things, that of not existing.

Returning late the other night from the room of
a friend in Victoria, I found myself walking
rapidly up Sloane Street in a small thinnish rain.
It must have been midnight or some such later
hour. Not a soul save my own made a way home up
that dead street or stood sheltering in a doorway
or strolled along arm in arm with another. The
electric street lamps hissed as the rain fell on them,
the little decorated towers and cupolas of hotels,
visible between clouds, took on the appearance of
an Austrian University town or palaces in a
Hungarian faery story. I think there were some trees, for
out of shadows that had, as I remember, the
conspiratorial patternings of a small wood,
out of this darkness, soundlessly, a large black dog
loped up beside me as I strode the pavement.
This beast then fell in, so to say, behind me, and
tracked me step by step like a hunter's hound.
I thought: this is a creature as lost, really, as I am.
But when I turned, as I could not help turning,
I saw that it grinned up at me with a look of
fear and a sort of knowing malice. I lengthened my step
and the brute broke into a trot. I hurried and
it began to gallop after me faster and faster.
The rain flew off its long black furry coat and
it seemed to glow mauve as it leaped along in the
electric lamplight. I heard it like a hog behind me
snuffling and I knew that I was pursued in midnight
by what a second person would have thought a dog.
As it grunted and hissed behind me I heard like a shaking
of metal and glass a late bus approaching
up the black street. It grew large like an illuminated

illusion and as it reached the strange pair of us
I sprang desperately at its entrance like an ambulance
as it passed. There was no one on this bus save
the Cockney conductor. 'You do that kind of thing
again,' he said, 'and you're for the big jump.
What about your dog?'

LIII

(*for my students at Wisconsin University*)

i

How can the ships at midnight
pass in a howling and
outrageous darkness without a
wave or shake of the hand
across the years and silences
that stretch like seas between
lips as they speak and words that
die upon what they mean?

ii

My hand upon your shoulder
as I stand here beside
you seated at the window
with your head turned aside
to watch the outstaying welcome
winter snows as they pass –
Rod Clark, a little love may
well come up with the grass.

iii

Lily and Lois, there's little
reasonable evidence
that the world makes common or
even uncommon sense, –
but, leaving out the angels
and the lost paradise,
since it's the only one we've got, –
it's worth its price?

Frisky the silly squirrels
   darting on Willow Drive
in spite of General Motors
   have learned how to survive.
Greg, with my own ears I have
   listened to little birds
utter in May things just as clear
   as I can say in words.

v

The white boats on Mendota
   caught in a summer squall
lean over and scud sideways
   then suddenly and to all
appearances disappear in
   the flying walls of rain, –
my dear Richard, they emerge
   and shake their wings again.

vi

The leaves of marijuana
   may turn in time to dust,
the dry Professors also
   if Justice is still just.
And your most creative concepts
   may, like the True Church, rot:
so, Woody, spend freely all the
   life and money you've got.

vii

And you, Mary, whose whitewashed
   face of the living dead
like an enamelled ikon stared
   at truths over my head,

you in your evergreen shadows most
of all must know and see
the heart from darkness rises up like
roses out of the sea.

LIV

The words are always as
strange and dead as those
fragments and oddments that
the wave casts up on the shore:
I stand in the sea mist
gazing down at the white
words and old bits of wood
and wonder what they were for.

I think that they were not
ever intended to do
what, when we seek to speak,
we believe that they may:
they cannot bear us up
the frothy words and like
wings at the lame foot
lift us out of the clay.

For all the reflections
I call up out of the sea
(they seem to speak as the shell
seems to speak for the sea)
are no more truly here
than the wind weaving sand
into the shapes of things
we think that we know and see.

When in the evening sky
a single star appears
over my head, and the moon
out of cloud lifts its face,
when the white gull turns

or the high plover hovers
to tell me with a cry
I trespass in this place:

What I see, then, with
that cloud my witness is
not shapes of the mind or wind
like the slow rainbowings
of the dolphin's skin as it dies
but, as though from the cloud
I saw my bone walk the shore,
the theology of all things.

The white stones and the old
odd bits of sea blanched wood,
Overstrand and the swinging
lighthouse glimpsed in the mists,
they flash in the prisms and I
believe for a moment I see
the dazzling atoms dancing
in every thing that exists.

The children dance on the shore.
The waves die on the sand.
The spray blows to and fro,
the children dance and die.
What waves are these that dance
with the children on the sand?
I hear them calling, but cannot
hear what it is that they cry.

I neither understand
or know why I am moved
beyond these words by the
odd bits of bleached wood

cast up on Overstrand
or by the black and twisted
October evening tree
dying beside the road

or by the child of midnight
so deep asleep but still
lost in the corridors
of the mansions of dust,
by any or by all
ceremonial evidence
attesting that we love
simply because we must.

I walk upon Overstrand shore
and the crab at my foot
inscribes praise in the sand.
The wave bursts with glory
because it rises up like
angels out of the sea,
and the dead starfish burns
on Overstrand promontory.

Why do I hear them cry
out from the far side of life,
those forms and impulses
unborn beyond the sky?
Why should they hope and seek
above all else to be?
Tonight on Overstrand
I know for one moment why.

The critic may sit down and, illuminated by the
dying sun of hindsight, observe those efforts
to communicate of men alone on rocks or drowning
daily in wilder seas, or clinging to the shipwreck
of their private lives, but what such men are seeking
to communicate to one another, this is
what the critic, having sat down in Canute's chair,
gets all wrong.

Men going under for the third time do not signal.
All signals by then are useless. When Paddy Finucane
spoke from his burning fighter as it spun:
'This is it, chaps' I know in my heart and
in my head that this marvellous message
is superior to any silence. The authenticity
of death forced him to utter a great judgement.
This was the voice of the absolutely alone man
seeking to circumvent that loneliness in
the only way we can: by crying out.
Sometimes the cry may be, as with the mad man,
a hyena howl, but it is still the cry. Sometimes
it may be the silence of the poet as he dies under
the hands of a Greek colonel. This silence says:
I, too, am human, and I can die without speaking.
Or this cry may be the muttering of the intellect
writing the line: 'I gotta use words when
I talk to you.'

For this silence is what the powers of darkness
seek to impose upon us, as they have always sought
to do, till we become like men sitting around
dumbfounded after a great natural disaster. This is

the silence of Sam Beckett, and a noble silence
it is too. But it is not final. It is the silence
of the paralysed spiritual system, struck dumb by the
obvious monstrosity of all things. It is the triumph
of the dark powers. Out of it, out of
this quite appalling silence, we await the
re-affirmation of a logos. It is possible
that this re-affirmation may be made by the computer
XKXKXK. We will know, then, we have inheritors.
For we have invented – and murdered – a god we
     could not discover.
Have we invented a successor whose destiny
it is to silence us? We have not died until we
are perfectly silent. 'This is it, chaps.' The rest
is the dialogues of memories and machines.

Every generation dies, providing one thing:
that it has lived. The crisis of the word,
the defeat of simply rational speech, is what
the poem takes off in flight from. I cry
but what do I cry? Just as the Indian fakir
sits on the banks of the Ganges repeating silently
to himself the single word: No, – so the intellect
of Europe sits on the banks of rational aggrandisement
disbelieving all things, and repeats the same word.
But speak the word it does, if only to itself.
There is no crisis of the word. There is a crisis
of the intellect and of the intellectual.
It is the crisis that precedes the acknowledgement
of the imperative of veneration. When speech ceases
to be seen and heard and understood as holy
it proceeds to invent its own deities, and these
can be distinguished by their clay feet. The dictionary
is the book of the intellect, and there is one thing
wrong with it. It is not aware that it is holy.

The intellect is the book of the man, and there is one
    thing
wrong with it. It has forgotten that it is holy.

Last of the Aldersons
lie, gentle murderer, quiet now
and let the bastards rage
and roar and riot now:

may only the cold rain
upon your burnt out fever
fall and calm the glowing
of your ashes for ever.

Sleep. Sleep. Obey
that heavenly verb you
followed into the grave.
May nothing ever disturb you.